Java 17 Quick Syntax Reference

A Pocket Guide to the Java SE Language, APIs, and Library

Third Edition

Mikael Olsson

Apress®

Java 17 Quick Syntax Reference: A Pocket Guide to the Java SE Language, APIs, and Library

Mikael Olsson
Hammarland, Länsi-Suomi, Finland

ISBN-13 (pbk): 978-1-4842-7370-8
https://doi.org/10.1007/978-1-4842-7371-5

ISBN-13 (electronic): 978-1-4842- 7371-5

Managing Director, Apress Media LLC: Welmoed Spahr
Acquisitions Editor: Steve Anglin
Development Editor: Matthew Moodie
Coordinating Editor: Mark Powers

Cover designed by eStudioCalamar

Cover image by Janco Ferlic on Unsplash (www.unsplash.com)

Distributed to the book trade worldwide by Apress Media, LLC, 1 New York Plaza, New York, NY 10004, U.S.A. Phone 1-800-SPRINGER, fax (201) 348-4505, e-mail orders-ny@springer-sbm.com, or visit www.springeronline.com. Apress Media, LLC is a California LLC and the sole member (owner) is Springer Science + Business Media Finance Inc (SSBM Finance Inc). SSBM Finance Inc is a **Delaware** corporation.

For information on translations, please e-mail booktranslations@springernature.com; for reprint, paperback, or audio rights, please e-mail bookpermissions@springernature.com.

Apress titles may be purchased in bulk for academic, corporate, or promotional use. eBook versions and licenses are also available for most titles. For more information, reference our Print and eBook Bulk Sales web page at http://www.apress.com/bulk-sales.

Any source code or other supplementary material referenced by the author in this book is available to readers on GitHub via the book's product page, located at www.apress.com/ 9781484273708. For more detailed information, please visit http://www.apress.com/ source-code.

Printed on acid-free paper

Table of Contents

About the Author

Mikael Olsson is a professional web entrepreneur, programmer, and author. He works for an R&D company in Finland where he specializes in software development. In his spare time, he writes books and creates websites that summarize various fields of interest. The books he writes are focused on teaching their subject in the most efficient way possible, by explaining only what is relevant and practical without any unnecessary repetition or theory.

About the Technical Reviewer

Manuel Jordan Elera is an autodidactic developer and researcher who enjoys learning new technologies for his own experiments and creating new integrations. Manuel won the Springy Award – Community Champion and Spring Champion 2013. In his little free time, he reads the Bible and composes music on his guitar. Manuel is known as dr_pompeii. He has tech-reviewed numerous books for Apress, including *Pro Spring MVC with WebFlux* (2020), *Pro Spring Boot 2* (2019), *Rapid Java Persistence and Microservices* (2019), *Java Language Features* (2018), *Spring Boot 2 Recipes* (2018), and *Java APIs, Extensions and Libraries* (2018). Read his 13 detailed tutorials about many Spring technologies, contact him through his blog at www.manueljordanelera.blogspot.com, and follow him on his Twitter account, @dr_pompeii.

Introduction

Java is a high-level object-oriented programming language developed by Sun Microsystems, which became part of Oracle Corporation in 2010. The language is very similar to C++ but has been simplified to make it easier to write bug-free code. Most notably, unlike C++, there are no pointers in Java—instead, all memory allocation and deallocation is handled automatically.

Despite simplifications like this, Java has considerably more functionality than C++, due to its large class library. Java programs also have high performance and can be made very secure, which has contributed to making Java the most popular general-purpose programming language in use today.

Another key feature of Java is that it is platform independent. This is achieved by only compiling programs halfway, into platform-independent instructions called *bytecode*. The bytecode is then interpreted, or run, by the Java Virtual Machine (JVM). That means any system that has this program and its accompanying libraries installed can run Java applications.

To allow Java to be used in a variety of environments, there are four different editions: Java ME, Java SE, Java EE, and Java FX. Each edition contains a JVM and a set of class libraries. Java SE (Standard Edition) provides the standard JVM along with the commonly used libraries for building applications, in particular desktop applications. Java ME (Micro Edition) is a small-footprint version of Java SE designed for running on small devices such as mobile phones. Java EE (Enterprise Edition) is an extended version of Java SE that includes libraries for building large-scale web applications. The most recently added edition is JavaFX, a lightweight version intended for building desktop and rich web applications. This edition includes a new library for making graphical user interfaces (GUIs), which is intended to replace the standard GUI library called Swing used in Java SE.

To allow Java to be used in a variety of environments, there are four different editions: Java SE, Java ME, Java EE, and Java FX. Each edition contains a JVM and a set of class libraries. Java SE (Standard Edition) provides the standard JVM along with the commonly used libraries for building applications, in particular desktop applications. Java ME (Micro Edition) is a small-footprint version of Java SE designed for running on small devices such as mobile phones. Java EE (Enterprise Edition) is an extended version of Java SE that includes libraries for building large-scale web applications. The most recently added edition is Java FX, a lightweight version intended for building rich web applications.

The Java language and class libraries have undergone major changes since their initial release in 1996. The naming conventions for the versions have gone through a few revisions as well, mainly for marketing reasons. The major releases include JDK 1.0, JDK 1.1, J2SE 1.2, J2SE 1.3, J2SE 1.4, J2SE 5.0, followed by Java SE 6 to Java SE 17, with Java SE 17 being the current version as of writing. For the sake of simplicity, the Java versions will be referred to as Java 1–17 in this book. Note that Java is designed to be backward-compatible. Therefore, the Virtual Machine for Java 17 can still run Java 1 applications.

CHAPTER 1

Hello World

Installing

Before you can program in Java, you need to download and install a Java Development Kit (JDK), such as the Standard Edition (JDK SE) from Oracle's website.[1] Among other things, the JDK includes the Java compiler, the class libraries, and the virtual machine needed to run Java applications. You should also download an Integrated Development Environment (IDE) as it will make development in Java much easier. One such Java IDE is Apache NetBeans,[2] which is available for free on Windows, macOS, and Linux. If you don't want to use any IDE at all, using a regular text editor is also an option. To work without an IDE, you can create an empty file with the .java extension—for example, MyApp.java—and open it in your text editor of choice.

Creating a Project

If you decide to use an IDE (recommended), you need to create a project, which will manage the Java source files and other resources. To create a project in NetBeans, click File ➤ New Project. In the dialog

---

[1] www.oracle.com/java/technologies/javase-downloads.html
[2] https://netbeans.org

© Mikael Olsson 2022
M. Olsson, *Java 17 Quick Syntax Reference*, https://doi.org/10.1007/978-1-4842-7371-5_1

box, select the Java Application project under the Java with Ant category, and click Next. In this dialog box, set the project name to "MyProject" and the name of the main class to "myproject.MyApp". Change the project's location if you want, and click Finish to generate the project. The project's only file, MyApp.java, will then open up, containing some default code. You can go ahead and remove all of that code so that you start with an empty source file.

Hello World

When you have your project and programming environment set up, the first application you will create is the Hello World program. This program will teach you how to compile and run Java applications, as well as how to output a string to a command window.

The first step in creating this program is to add a public class to your MyApp.java source file. The class must have the same name as the physical source file without the file extension—in this case, "MyApp." It's legal to have more than one class per file in Java, but only one public class is allowed, and its name must match the filename. Keep in mind that Java is case sensitive. The curly brackets following the class name delimit what belongs to the class and must be included. The brackets, along with their content, are referred to as a *code block*, or just a *block*.

```
public class MyApp {}
```

Java classes are organized into packages, which are similar to namespaces in other languages. A package statement needs to appear at the top of the file to designate which package a file belongs to. This name must match the directory the file is located in relative to the project's source directory, so in this case, the package name is myproject.

```
package myproject;
public class MyApp {}
```

Next, add the main method inside the class. This is the starting point of the application and must always be included in the same form as is shown in the following code. The keywords themselves will be examined in later chapters.

```
package myproject;
public class MyApp {
  public static void main(String[] args) {}
}
```

The last step in completing the Hello World program is to output the text by calling the print method. This method is located inside the System class and then another level down inside the out class. The method takes a single argument—the string to be printed—and it ends with a semicolon, as do all statements in Java.

```
package myproject;
public class MyApp {
  public static void main(String[] args) {
    System.out.print("Hello World");
  }
}
```

Note that the dot operator (.) is used to access members of a class. Similar to print, there's also the println method, which automatically adds a line break at the end of the printed string. The System class belongs to the java.lang package, which is always included in a Java project.

Code Hints

If you're unsure of what a specific class contains, or what arguments a method takes, you can take advantage of code hints in some IDEs, such as NetBeans. The code hint window appears anytime you're typing code, and there are multiple predetermined alternatives. You can also bring it up manually by pressing Ctrl+spacebar. This is a powerful feature that gives you quick access to the class libraries and their members, along with descriptions.

CHAPTER 2

Compile and Run

Running from the IDE

With your Hello World program complete, you can compile and run it in one of two ways. The first method is by selecting Run from the menu bar of the IDE you're using. In NetBeans, the menu command is Run ➤ Run Project. The IDE will then compile and run the application, which displays the text "Hello World" in the output window of the IDE.

Running from a Console Window

The other way is to manually compile the program using a console window, such as C:\Windows\System32\cmd.exe under Windows. The most convenient way to do this is to first add the JDK bin directory to the PATH environment variable. In Windows, you do this using the SET PATH command and then by appending the path to your JDK installation's bin folder separated by a semicolon. Note that the exact path depends on what version of the JDK you have installed.

```
SET PATH=%PATH%;"C:\Program Files\Java\jdk-17.0.2\bin"
```

By doing this, the console will be able to find the Java compiler from any folder for the duration of this console session. The PATH variable can also be permanently changed.[1] Next, navigate to the folder where the Java source file is located, and run the compiler by typing *javac* followed by the complete filename.

```
C:\MyProject\src\myproject> javac MyApp.java
```

The program will be compiled into a class file called MyApp.class. This class file contains bytecode instead of machine code, so to execute it, you need to call the Java Virtual Machine by typing *java* followed by the fully qualified class name, which includes the package name. This command needs to be executed from the parent folder, the project's source folder. Notice that the .java extension is used when compiling a file, but the .class extension is not used when running it.

```
C:\MyProject\src> java myproject.MyApp
```

Alternatively, as of Java 11, you can both compile and run the source file by giving the complete filename to the java command:

```
java MyApp.java
```

Comments

Comments are used to insert notes into the source code and have no effect on the end program. Java has the standard C++ comment notation, with both single-line and multi-line comments.

```
// single-line comment
```

```
/* multi-line
   comment */
```

---

[1] www.java.com/en/download/help/path.xml

In addition to these, there is the Javadoc comment. This comment is used to generate documentation by using a utility included in the JDK bin folder, which is also called Javadoc.

```
/** javadoc
    comment */
```

Preview Features

A preview feature is a new feature that is subject to change in future JDK releases. To compile code that contains preview features, you must specify an additional command-line option for your project. In NetBeans, this is done by first opening the File ➤ Project Properties window. From there, select the Compiling tab from the Build category, and at the bottom of this window, add "--enable-preview" in the input box labeled "Additional Compiler Options". Click OK, and preview features will be enabled for this project.

CHAPTER 3

Variables

Variables are used for storing data in memory during program execution.

Data Types

Depending on what data you need to store, there are several kinds of data types. Java has eight types built into the language, called *primitives*. The integer (whole number) types are byte, short, int, and long. The float and double types represent floating-point numbers (real numbers). The char type holds a Unicode character, and the boolean type contains either a true or false value. Except for these primitive types, every other type in Java is represented by a class, an interface, or an array.

Data Type	Size (Bits)	Description
byte	8	Signed integer
short	16	
int	32	
long	64	
float	32	Floating-point number
double	64	
char	16	Unicode character
boolean	1	Boolean value

© Mikael Olsson 2022
M. Olsson, *Java 17 Quick Syntax Reference*, https://doi.org/10.1007/978-1-4842-7371-5_3

Declaring Variables

To declare (create) a variable, you start with the data type you want it to hold followed by a variable name. The name can be anything you want, but it's a good idea to give your variables names that are closely related to the values they will hold. The standard naming convention for variables is that the first word should be lowercase and any subsequent words initially capitalized.

```
int myInt;
```

Assigning Variables

To give the variable a value, you use the assignment operator (=) followed by the value. When a variable is initialized (assigned a value), it then becomes defined (declared and assigned).

```
myInt = 10;
```

The declaration and assignment can be combined into a single statement:

```
int myInt = 10;
```

If you need multiple variables of the same type, there is a shorthand way of declaring or defining them using the comma operator (,):

```
int myInt = 10, myInt2 = 20, myInt3;
```

Using Variables

Once a variable has been defined, you can use it by simply referencing the variable's name—for example, to print it:

```
System.out.print(myInt);
```

Integer Types

As shown earlier, there are four signed integer types you can use, depending on how large a number you need the variable to hold:

```
byte  myInt8  = 2;  // -128   to +127
short myInt16 = 1;  // -32768 to +32767
int   myInt32 = 0;  // -2^31  to +2^31-1
long  myInt64 = -1; // -2^63  to +2^63-1
```

In addition to standard decimal notation, integers can also be assigned by using octal or hexadecimal notation. As of Java 7, a binary notation is also available.

```
int myHex = 0xF;  // hexadecimal (base 16)
int myOct = 07;   // octal (base 8)
int myBin = 0b10; // binary (base 2)
```

Digits in a number can be separated by an underscore (_). This feature was introduced in Java 7 and is provided only to improve readability.

```
int bigNumber = 10_000_000;
```

Floating-Point Types

The floating-point types can store integers as well as floats. They can be assigned with either decimal or exponential notation.

```
double myDouble = 3.14;
double myDouble2 = 3e2; // 3*10^2 = 300
```

11

Note that constant floating-point numbers in Java are always kept internally as doubles. Therefore, if you try to assign a double to a float, you'll get an error because a double has a higher precision than a float. To assign it correctly, you can append an *F* character to the constant, which says that the number is in fact a float.

```
float myFloat = 3.14;   // error
float myFloat = 3.14F; // ok
```

A more common and useful way to do that is by using an explicit cast. An *explicit cast* is performed by placing the desired data type in parentheses before the variable or constant that is to be converted. This will convert the value to the specified type—in this case, float—before the assignment occurs.

```
float myFloat = (float)3.14;
```

Char Type

The char data type can contain a single Unicode character, delimited by single quotes:

```
char myChar = 'A';
```

Chars can also be assigned by using a special hexadecimal notation that gives access to all Unicode characters:

```
char myChar = '\u0000'; // \u0000 to \uFFFF
```

Boolean Type

The boolean type can store a Boolean value, which is a value that can only be either true or false. These values are specified with the true and false keywords.

```
boolean myBool = false;
```

12

Variable Scope

The *scope* of a variable refers to the code block within which it's possible to use that variable without qualification. For example, a *local variable* is a variable declared within a method. Such a variable will only be available within the method's code block, after it's been declared. Once the scope (code block) of the method ends, the local variable will be destroyed.

```java
public static void main(String[] args)
{
  int localVar; // local variable
}
```

In addition to local variables, Java has field- and parameter-type variables, which later chapters will cover. But Java doesn't have global variables, as, for example, C++ does.

Anonymous Block

You can restrict the scope of local variables using an *anonymous* (unnamed) code block. This construct is seldom used, because if a method is large enough to warrant the use of an anonymous block, a better choice is often to break up the code into separate methods.

```java
public static void main(String[] args)
{
  // Anonymous code block
  {
    int localVar = 10;
  }
  // localVar is unavailable from here
}
```

Type Inference

Beginning with Java 10, local variables can be declared with *var* to have the compiler automatically determine the type of the variable based on its assignment. The following two declarations are therefore equivalent:

```
var i = 5; // Implicit type
int i = 5; // Explicit type
```

When to use var comes down to preference. In cases when the type of the variable is obvious from the assignment, use of var may be preferable to shorten the declaration and improve readability. The benefit becomes more apparent when using a non-primitive type as seen in this example.

```
// No type inference
java.util.ArrayList a = new java.util.ArrayList();

// With type inference
var a = new java.util.ArrayList();
```

Keep in mind that var can only be used when a local variable is both declared and initialized at the same time.

CHAPTER 4

Operators

Operators are special symbols used to operate on values. The operators that deal specifically with numbers can be grouped into five types: arithmetic, assignment, comparison, logical, and bitwise operators.

Arithmetic Operators

The arithmetic operators include the four basic arithmetic operations, as well as the modulus operator (%), which is used to obtain the division remainder:

```
float x = 3+2; // addition (5)
      x = 3-2; // subtraction (1)
      x = 3*2; // multiplication (6)
      x = 3/2; // division (1)
      x = 3%2; // modulus (1)
```

Note that the division sign gives an incorrect result. That's because it operates on two integer values and will therefore round the result and return an integer. To get the correct value, one of the numbers must be explicitly converted to a floating-point type.

```
float x = (float)3/2; // 1.5
```

© Mikael Olsson 2022
M. Olsson, *Java 17 Quick Syntax Reference*, https://doi.org/10.1007/978-1-4842-7371-5_4

Assignment Operators

The second group is the assignment operators—most importantly, the assignment operator itself (=), which assigns a value to a variable:

```
int i = 0; // assignment
```

A common use of the assignment and arithmetic operators is to operate on a variable and then save the result back into that same variable. These operations can be shortened with the combined assignment operators.

```
i += 5; // i = i+5;
i -= 5; // i = i-5;
i *= 5; // i = i*5;
i /= 5; // i = i/5;
i %= 5; // i = i%5;
```

Increment and Decrement Operators

Another common operation is to increment or decrement a variable by one. This can be simplified with the increment (++) and decrement (−−) operators.

```
++i; // i = i+1
--i; // i = i-1
```

Both of these can be used either before or after a variable:

```
++i; // pre-increment
--i; // pre-decrement
i++; // post-increment
i--; // post-decrement
```

The result on the variable is the same whichever is used. The difference is that the post-operator returns the original value before it changes the variable, while the pre-operator changes the variable first and then returns the value.

```
int x, y;
x = 5; y = x++; // y=5, x=6
x = 5; y = ++x; // y=6, x=6
```

Comparison Operators

The comparison operators compare two values and return either true or false. They're mainly used to specify *conditions*, which are expressions that evaluate to either true or false.

```
boolean b = (2==3); // equal to (false)
        b = (2!=3); // not equal to (true)
        b = (2>3);  // greater than (false)
        b = (2<3);  // less than (true)
        b = (2>=3); // greater than or equal to (false)
        b = (2<=3); // less than or equal to (true)
```

Logical Operators

The logical operators are often used together with the comparison operators. Logical *and* (&&) evaluates to true if both the left and right side are true, and logical *or* (||) is true if either the left or right side is true. For inverting a Boolean result, there is a logical *not* (!) operator. Note that for both logical *and* and logical *or*, the right-hand side won't be evaluated if the result is already determined by the left-hand side.

```
boolean b = (true && false); // logical and (false)
        b = (true || false); // logical or (true)
        b = !(true);         // logical not (false)
```

Bitwise Operators

The bitwise operators can manipulate individual bits inside an integer type. For example, the right shift operator (>>) moves all bits except the sign bit to the right, whereas zero-fill right shift (>>>) moves all bits right including the sign bit.

```
byte b = 5 & 4;   // 101 & 100 = 100 (4) // and
     b = 5 | 4;   // 101 | 100 = 101 (5) // or
     b = 5 ^ 4;   // 101 ^ 100 = 001 (1) // xor
     b = 4 << 1;  // 100 << 1 = 1000 (8) // left shift
     b = 4 >> 1;  // 100 >> 1 = 10 (2) // right shift
     b = 4 >>>1;  // 100 >>>1 = 10 (2) // zero-fill right shift
     b = ~4;      // ~00000100 = 11111011 (-5) // invert
```

These bitwise operators have shorthand assignment operators, just like the arithmetic operators:

```
int i = 5;
   i &= 4;    // "and" and assign
   i |= 4;    // or and assign
   i ^= 4;    // xor and assign
   i <<= 1;   // left shift and assign
   i >>= 1;   // right shift and assign
   i >>>= 1;  // right shift and assign (move sign bit)
```

Operator Precedence

In Java, expressions are normally evaluated from left to right. However, when an expression contains multiple operators, the precedence of those operators decides the order that they're evaluated in. The order of precedence is shown in the following table. This same order also applies to many other languages, such as C++ and C#.

Precedence	Operator	Precedence	Operator
1	++ −− ! ~	7	&
2	* / %	8	^
3	+ −	9	|
4	<< >> >>>	10	&&
5	< <= > >=	11	||
6	== !=	12	= operator=

For example, logical *and* (&&) binds weaker than relational operators, which in turn bind weaker than arithmetic operators:

```
boolean b = 2+3 > 1*4 && 5/5 == 1; // true
```

To avoid having to learn the precedents of all operators, and to clarify the intent, you can use parentheses to specify which part of the expression will be evaluated first:

```
boolean b = ( (2+3) > (1*4) ) && ( (5/5) == 1 ); // true
```

CHAPTER 5

String

The String class in Java is a data type that can hold string literals. *String* is a reference data type, as are all non-primitive data types. This means that the variable contains an address to an object in the memory and not the object itself. A String object is created in the memory, and the address to the object is returned to the variable. As seen in the following code, string literals are delimited by double quotes:

```
String a = "Hello";
```

String literals are stored in the so-called String pool, maintained by the String class. For performance reasons, any string literal that is equal to a previously created string will refer to the same String object in the pool. This works because strings in Java are immutable and therefore cannot be changed without creating a new String object.

```
String a1 = "Hello";
String a2 = "Hello"; // refers to same object as a1
```

Combining Strings

The plus sign is used to combine two strings. Known as the *concatenation* operator (+) in this context, it has an accompanying assignment operator (+=) that appends one string to another and creates a new string.

```
String a = "Hello";
String b = " World";
```

© Mikael Olsson 2022

M. Olsson, *Java 17 Quick Syntax Reference*, https://doi.org/10.1007/978-1-4842-7371-5_5

```
String c = a+b; // "Hello World"
       a += b;  // "Hello World"
```

Note that although a statement may be divided into multiple lines, a string must be on a single row unless it's split up using the concatenation operator:

```
String x
      = "Hello " +
        "World";
```

Escape Characters

For adding new lines to the string itself, there is the escape character (\n). This backslash notation is used to write special characters, such as backslash and double quotes. Among the special characters is also a Unicode character notation for writing any character. All the escape characters can be seen in the following table.

Character	Meaning
\n	Newline
\t	Horizontal tab
\b	Backspace
\r	Carriage return
\uFFFF	Unicode character(four-digit hex number)
\f	Form feed
\'	Single quote
\"	Double quotes
\\	Backslash

String Compare

The way to compare two strings is to use the equals method of the String class. If the equality operator (==) is used, the memory addresses will be compared instead.

```
boolean x = a.equals(b); // compares string
boolean y = (a == b);    // compares address
```

Bear in mind that all strings in Java are String objects. Therefore, it's possible to call methods directly on constant strings, just as it is on variables.

```
boolean z = "Hello".equals(a); // true
```

StringBuffer Class

The String class has a large number of methods available, but it doesn't contain any methods for manipulating strings. That's because strings in Java are immutable. Once a String object has been created, the contents can't be changed unless the whole string is completely replaced. Because most strings are never modified, this was done on purpose to make the String class more efficient. For cases when you need a modifiable string, you can use the StringBuffer class, which is a mutable string object.

```
StringBuffer sb = new StringBuffer("Hello");
```

This class has several methods to manipulate strings, including append, delete, and insert:

```
sb.append(" World");    // add to end of string
sb.delete(0, 5);        // remove 5 first characters
sb.insert(0, "Hello"); // insert string at beginning
```

23

You can convert a `StringBuffer` object back into a regular string with the `toString` method, which returns a string representation of the object. It exists for every class in Java, because it's defined by `Object`, which is inherited by all classes.

```
String s = sb.toString();
```

Text Blocks

A text block is a multi-line string delimited by three double quotes (`"""`). It provides a simplified way to write a string that spans more than one line without having to specify escape characters, such as newlines or quotes.

```
String textBlock = """
line 1
line 2""";
```

The line break after the opening delimiter is mandatory, so a text block must span more than one line. Any line break used within a text block will automatically be interpreted as a newline character, so the previous text block is equivalent to the following string:

```
String s = "line 1\nline 2";
```

Whitespace that indents one line of text relative to other lines will be kept. However, any initial whitespace used to indent all lines will be removed.

```
String html = """
            <div>
              <p>Hi</p>
            </div>""";
```

This text block is therefore identical to the following string:

```
String html = "<div>\n  <p>Hi</p>\n</div>";
```

Text blocks were introduced as a preview feature in Java 13 and became a standard feature as of Java 15.

CHAPTER 6

Arrays

An *array* is a fixed-size data structure used for storing a collection of values of a single type.

Array Declaration

To declare an array, a set of square brackets is appended to the data type the array will contain, followed by the array's name. Arrays can be declared with any data type, and all of its elements must then be of that type.

```
int[] x;
```

Alternatively, the brackets may be placed after the array name. However, this form is discouraged. Since the brackets affect the type, they should appear next to the type.

```
int y[]; // discouraged form
```

Array Allocation

The array is allocated with the new keyword, followed again by the data type and a set of square brackets containing the *length* of the array—the fixed number of elements the array can contain. Once the array is created, the elements will automatically be assigned to the default values for that data type, which is zero (0) in the case of an int array.

```
int[] y = new int[3]; // allocate 3 elements with value 0
```

© Mikael Olsson 2022
M. Olsson, *Java 17 Quick Syntax Reference*, https://doi.org/10.1007/978-1-4842-7371-5_6

Array Assignment

To fill the array, elements can be referenced one at a time by placing the element's numerical index inside the square brackets and then assigning them values. Notice that the index starts with zero.

```
y[0] = 1;
y[1] = 2;
y[2] = 3;
```

Alternatively, the values can be assigned all at once using a curly bracket notation. The new keyword, data type, and square brackets may be optionally left out if the array is declared at the same time.

```
int[] x = new int[] {1,2,3};
int[] x = {1,2,3};
```

Once the array elements are initialized, they can be accessed by referencing the elements' indexes inside the square brackets:

```
System.out.print(x[0] + x[1] + x[2]); // "6"
```

Multidimensional Arrays

Multidimensional arrays are declared, created, and initialized like one-dimensional arrays, except that they have additional square brackets. They can have any number of dimensions, and for each dimension, another set of square brackets is added.

```
String[][] x = {{"00","01"},{"10","11"}};
String[][] y = new String[2][2];
```

```
y[0][0] = "00";
y[0][1] = "01";
y[1][0] = "10";
y[1][1] = "11";

System.out.print(x[0][0] + x[1][1]); // "0011"
```

ArrayList Class

Something important to keep in mind about arrays is that their length is fixed and there's no way to change their size. The size of an array can be retrieved through the length member of the array.

```
Int[] x = new int[3];
int size = x.length; // 3
```

For cases when a resizable array is needed, the generic ArrayList<T> class can be used, which is located in the java.util package. The data type that this list will hold is specified inside the angle brackets (<>). Generic classes will be looked at in more detail in later chapters.

```
import java.util.ArrayList;
// ...
// Create an ArrayList collection for strings
java.util.ArrayList<String> a = new java.util.ArrayList<>();
```

The ArrayList class has several useful methods to change the list, such as add, set, and remove:

```
a.add("Hi"); // add an element
a.set(0, "Hello"); // change first element
a.remove(0); // remove first element
```

To retrieve an element from the ArrayList<T>, you use the get method. The element then has to be explicitly cast back to its original type, because it is stored internally as the Object type, which can to hold any reference data type.

```
a.add("Hello World");
String s = (String)a.get(0); // Hello World
```

CHAPTER 7

Conditionals

Conditional statements are used to execute different code blocks based on different conditions.

If Statement

The `if` statement will only execute if the condition inside the parentheses is evaluated to true. The condition can include any of the comparison and logical operators.

```java
int x = 1;
// ...
if (x == 1) {
  System.out.println(x + " = 1");
}
```

To test for other conditions, the `if` statement can be extended by any number of `else-if` clauses. Each additional condition will only be tested if all previous conditions are false.

```java
else if (x > 1) {
  System.out.println(x + " > 1");
}
```

© Mikael Olsson 2022
M. Olsson, *Java 17 Quick Syntax Reference*, https://doi.org/10.1007/978-1-4842-7371-5_7

For handling all other cases, there can be one `else` clause at the end, which executes if all previous conditions are false:

```java
else {
  System.out.println(x + " < 1");
}
```

The curly brackets can be left out if only a single statement needs to be executed conditionally. However, it is considered good practice to include them since they improve code readability.

```java
if (x == 1)
  System.out.println(x + " = 1");
else if (x > 1)
  System.out.println(x + " > 1");
else
  System.out.println(x + " < 1");
```

Switch Statement

The `switch` statement checks for equality between a value and a series of case labels. It then executes the matching case. The statement can contain any number of cases and may end with a default label for handling all other cases.

```java
switch (x)
{
  case 0:  System.out.println(x + " is 0"); break;
  case 1:  System.out.println(x + " is 1"); break;
  default: System.out.println(x + " is something else");
}
```

Note that the statements after each case label aren't surrounded by curly brackets. Instead, the statements end with the break keyword. Without the break, the execution will fall through to the next case. This can be useful if several cases need to be evaluated in the same way.

Any integer data type can be used with a switch statement, including byte, short, int, and char. As of Java 7, the String type is also permitted.

```java
String fruit = "apple";
switch (fruit)
{
  case "apple": System.out.println("apple"); break;
  default: System.out.println("not an apple");
}
```

Switch Expression

The switch was extended with new preview features in Java 12 that became standard features in Java 14. Consider the following switch which is used to simulate an expression (code that evaluates to a value):

```java
String result;
switch (x)
{
  case 1: result = "one"; break;
  case 2:
  case 3: result = "two or three"; break;
  default: result = "many";
}
```

This code can be made more concise using the arrow label (->) instead of the traditional case label. When using this form, only a single expression or statement may appear after the arrow label, and each case may include more than one constant, separated by commas. Arrow labels do not allow fall-throughs so the break keyword is not used.

```
String result;
switch (x)
{
  case 1  -> result = "one";
  case 2, 3  -> result = "two or three";
  default -> result = "many";
}
```

This switch statement can be further simplified by turning it into a switch expression. In this form, the switch will evaluate to the expression that follows the matching case. Keep in mind that the default label then becomes mandatory so that all possible input values result in a valid expression.

```
String result = switch (x)
{
  case 1   -> "one";
  case 2, 3  -> "two or three";
  default -> "many";
};
```

If more than one expression is needed, a full code block can be included. In such a block, the yield statement is used to specify the value that the switch expression will evaluate to.

```
String result = switch (x)
{
  case 1 -> "one";
```

```
  case 2, 3 -> "two or three";
  default -> {
    if (x == 4) yield "four";
    else yield "many";
  }
};
```

Ternary Operator

The ternary operator (?:) can replace a single if-else clause with a value to be returned. The operator takes three expressions. If the first one is evaluated to true, then the second expression is returned, but if it's false, the third one is evaluated and returned. It is the only operator in Java which accepts three operands.

```
x = (x < 0.5) ? 0 : 1; // ternary operator (?:)
```

This ternary statement is equivalent to the following if-else clause:

```
if (x < 0.5) { x = 0; }
else { x = 1; }
```

CHAPTER 8

Loops

There are four looping structures in Java. They're used to execute a specific code block multiple times. As with the conditional if statement, the curly brackets for the loops can be left out if there's only one statement in the code block.

While Loop

The while loop runs through the code block only if the specified condition is true and will continue looping for as long as the condition remains true. The following loop will print out the numbers 0 to 4:

```java
int i = 0;
while (i < 5) {
  System.out.print(i++); // "01234"
}
```

Note that the condition for the loop must evaluate to a boolean value. This condition is checked only at the start of each iteration (loop).

© Mikael Olsson 2022
M. Olsson, *Java 17 Quick Syntax Reference*, https://doi.org/10.1007/978-1-4842-7371-5_8

Do While Loop

The do while loop works the same way as the while loop, except that it checks the condition after the code block. It will therefore always run through the code block at least once.

```
int i = 0;
do {
  System.out.print(i++);
} while (i < 5); // "01234"
```

For Loop

The for loop is used to go through a code block a specific number of times. It uses three parameters. The first parameter initializes a counter and is always executed once, before the loop. This counter variable is limited in scope to the for loop and is not accessible after the loop. The second parameter holds the condition for the loop and is checked before each iteration. Lastly, the third parameter contains the increment of the counter and is executed at the end of each iteration.

```
for (int i = 0; i < 5; i++) {
  System.out.print(i); // "01234"
}
```

Several variations of the for loop are possible. For instance, the first and third parameters can be split into several statements using the comma operator.

```
for (int k = 0, m = 0; k < 5; k++, m--) {
  System.out.print(k + m); // "00000"
}
```

You also have the option of leaving out one or more of the parameters. For example, the third parameter can be moved into the body of the loop.

```
for (int k = 0, m = 0; k < 5;) {
  System.out.print(k + m); // "00000"
  k++; m--;
}
```

For Each Loop

The "for each" loop provides an easy way to iterate through arrays. On each iteration, the next element in the array is assigned to the specified variable, and the loop continues to execute until it has gone through the entire array.

```
int[] array = { 1,2,3 };
for (int element : array) {
  System.out.print(element); // "123"
}
```

Break and Continue

There are two special keywords that can be used inside loops: break and continue. The break keyword ends the loop structure, and continue skips the rest of the current iteration and continues at the beginning of the next iteration.

```
for (int i = 0; i < 10; i++)
{
  if (i == 5) break; // end loop
  if (i == 3) continue; // start next iteration
  System.out.print(i); // "0124"
}
```

To break out of a loop above the current one, that loop must first be labeled by adding a name followed by a colon before it. With this label in place, it can now be used as an argument to the break statement, telling it which loop to break out of. This also works with the continue keyword in order to skip to the next iteration of the named loop.

```
myLoop: for (int i = 0; i < 10; i++)
{
  for (int j = 0; j < 10; j++)
  {
    break myLoop; // end outer for loop
  }
}
```

Labeled Block

A *labeled* block, also called a *named* block, is created by placing a label before an anonymous code block. The break keyword can be used to break out of such a block, just as in labeled loops. This could be useful, for example, when performing a validation, where if one validation step fails, the whole process must be aborted.

```
validation:
{
  if(true)
    break validation;
}
```

Labeled blocks can be useful for organizing a large method into sections. In most cases, splitting the method up is a better idea. But if the new method would require a lot of parameters, or if the method would only be used from a single location, then one or more labeled blocks may be preferable.

CHAPTER 9

Methods

Methods are reusable code blocks that only execute when called.

Defining Methods

You can create a method by typing a return type followed by the method's name, a set of parentheses, and a code block. The void keyword can be used to specify that the method won't return a value. The naming convention for methods is the same as for variables—a descriptive name with the first word in lowercase and the first letter of any subsequent words capitalized.

```
class MyApp
{
  void myPrint()
  {
    System.out.println("Hello");
  }
}
```

© Mikael Olsson 2022
M. Olsson, *Java 17 Quick Syntax Reference*, https://doi.org/10.1007/978-1-4842-7371-5_9

Calling Methods

The preceding method will simply print out a text message. To *invoke* (call) it from the main method, an instance of the MyApp class must be created first. The dot operator is then used after the instance's name in order to access its members, which include the myPrint method.

```
public static void main(String[] args)
{
  MyApp m = new MyApp();
  m.myPrint(); // "Hello"
}
```

Method Parameters

The parentheses that follow the method name are used to pass arguments to the method. To do that, the corresponding parameters must first be added to the method declaration in the form of a comma-separated list.

```
void myPrint(String s)
{
  System.out.println(s);
}
```

A method can be defined to take any number of arguments, and they can have any data types. Just ensure that the method is called with the same types and number of arguments in the correct order.

```
public static void main(String[] args)
{
  MyApp m = new MyApp();
  m.myPrint("Hello"); // "Hello"
}
```

To be precise, *parameters* appear in method definitions, whereas *arguments* appear in method calls. However, the two terms are sometimes mistakenly used interchangeably.

Return Statement

A method can return a value. The void keyword is then replaced with the data type the method will return, and the return keyword is added to the method body with an argument of the specified return type.

```
public class MyApp
{
  String getString()
  {
    return "Hello";
  }
}
```

Return is a jump statement that causes the method to exit and return the specified value to the place where the method was called. For example, the preceding method can be passed as an argument to the println method because the method evaluates to a string.

```
public static void main(String[] args)
{
  MyApp m = new MyApp();
  System.out.println( m.getString() ); // "Hello"
}
```

The `return` statement can also be used in `void` methods to exit before the end block is reached. When used in this context, no return value is specified.

```
void myPrint(String s)
{
  if (s == "") { return; } // skip if string is empty
  System.out.println(s);
}
```

Method Overloading

It's possible to declare multiple methods with the same name as long as the parameters vary in type or number. Called *method overloading,* this can, for example, be seen in the implementation of the `System.out.println` method. It's a powerful feature that allows a method to handle a variety of arguments without the programmer needing to be aware of using different methods.

```
void myPrint(String s)
{
  System.out.println(s);
}

void myPrint(int i)
{
  System.out.println(i);
}
```

Passing Arguments

Java is different from many other languages in that all method parameters are passed by value. In fact, they can't be passed by reference. For value data types (primitive types), that means only a local copy of the variable is changed within the method, so the change won't affect the original variable. For reference data types (classes, interfaces, and arrays), it means only a copy of the memory address is passed to the method. Therefore, if the entire object is replaced, the change won't propagate back to the caller, but changes to the object will affect the original since the copy points to the same memory location.

```
public class MyApp
{
  public static void main(String[] args)
  {
    MyApp m = new MyApp();
    int x = 0;                 // value data type
    m.set(x);                  // value is passed
    System.out.println(x);     // "0"

    int[] y = {0};             // reference data type
    m.set(y);                  // address is passed
    System.out.println(y[0]); // "10"
  }

  void set(int a) { a = 10; }
  void set(int[] a) { a[0] = 10; }
}
```

CHAPTER 10

Class

A *class* is a template used to create objects. Classes are made up of members, the main two of which are fields and methods. *Fields* are variables that hold the state of the object, whereas *methods* define what the object can do—the so-called behaviors of the object.

```java
class MyRectangle
{
  int x, y;
  int getArea() { return x * y; }
}
```

Object Creation

To access a (non-static) field or method from outside the defining class, an object of the class must first be created. That's done using the new keyword, which will create a new object in the system's memory.

```java
public class MyApp
{
  public static void main(String[] args)
  {
    // Create an object of MyRectangle
    MyRectangle r = new MyRectangle();
  }
}
```

© Mikael Olsson 2022
M. Olsson, *Java 17 Quick Syntax Reference*, https://doi.org/10.1007/978-1-4842-7371-5_10

An object is also called an *instance*. The object will contain its own set of instance variables (non-static fields), which can hold values that are different from those of other instances of the class.

Accessing Object Members

In addition to creating the object, the members of the class that are to be accessible beyond their package need to be declared as public in the class definition.

```
class MyRectangle
{
  public int x, y;
  public int getArea() { return x * y; }
}
```

The members of this object can now be reached by using the dot operator after the instance name:

```
public class MyApp
{
  public static void main(String[] args)
  {
    MyRectangle r = new MyRectangle();
    r.x = 10;
    r.y = 5;
    int area = r.getArea(); // 50 (5*10)
  }
}
```

Constructor

A class can have a *constructor*, a special kind of method used to instantiate (construct) the object. It always has the same name as the class and doesn't have a return type, since it implicitly returns a new instance of the class. To be accessible from another class not in its package, it needs to be declared with the `public` access modifier. When a new instance of the `MyRectangle` class is created using the `new` syntax, the constructor method is called, which in the following example sets the fields to the specified default values.

```
class MyRectangle
{
  int x, y;
  public MyRectangle() { x = 10; y = 20; }
}
```

The constructor can have a parameter list, like any other method. As shown in the following code, this can be used to make the fields' initial values depend on the parameters passed when the object is created.

```
class MyRectangle
{
  int x, y;
  public MyRectangle(int a, int b) { x = a; y = b; }
}

public class MyApp
{
  public static void main(String[] args)
  {
    MyRectangle r = new MyRectangle(20, 15);
  }
}
```

This Keyword

Inside the constructor, as well as in other methods belonging to the object, a special keyword called *this* can be used. The this keyword is a reference to the current instance of the class. If, for example, the constructor's parameters have the same names as the corresponding instance variables, then the instance variables could still be accessed by using the this keyword, even though they're overshadowed by the parameters.

```
class MyRectangle
{
  int x, y;
  public MyRectangle(int x, int y)
  {
    this.x = x;
    this.y = y;
  }
}
```

Constructor Overloading

To support different parameter lists, the constructor can be overloaded. In the following example, if the class is instantiated without any parameters, the fields will be assigned the specified default values. With one parameter, both fields will be set to the supplied value, and with two parameters, each field will be assigned a separate value.

```
class MyRectangle
{
  int x, y;
  public MyRectangle()            { x = 10; y = 20; }
```

```
   public MyRectangle(int a)        { x = a;  y = a;  }
   public MyRectangle(int a, int b) { x = a;  y = b;  }
}
```

Attempting to create an object with the wrong number of arguments or with incorrect data types will result in a compile-time error, just as with any other method.

Constructor Chaining

You can also use the this keyword to call one constructor from another. Known as *constructor chaining*, this allows for greater code reuse. Note that the keyword appears as a method call and that it must be on the first line in the constructor.

```
public MyRectangle()            { this(10, 20); }
public MyRectangle(int a)       { this(a, a);   }
public MyRectangle(int a, int b) { x = a; y = b; }
```

Initial Field Values

If there are fields in the class that need to be assigned default values, such as in the first constructor just shown, the fields can simply be assigned at the same time as they are declared. These initial values will be assigned before the constructor is called.

```
class MyRectangle
{
   int x = 10, y = 20;
}
```

Default Constructor

It's possible to create a class even if no constructors are defined. That's because the compiler will then automatically create a default parameterless constructor.

```
public class MyApp
{
  public static void main(String[] args)
  {
    // Default constructor used
    MyApp a = new MyApp();
  }
}
```

If any custom constructor is defined, the default parameterless constructor will not be added by the compiler.

Null

The built-in constant null is used to represent an uninitialized object. It can only be assigned to objects and not to variables of primitive types. The equal-to operator (==) can be used to test whether an object is null.

```
String s = null;
// ...
if (s == null) s = new String();
```

Default Values

The default value of an object is null. For primitive data types, the
default values are as follows: integer types become 0, floating-point
types become 0.0, a char has the Unicode character for zero (\0000),
and a Boolean is false. Default values will be automatically assigned
by the compiler, but only for fields and not for local variables. However,
explicitly specifying the default value for fields is considered good
programming because it makes the code easier to understand. For local
variables, the default values aren't set by the compiler. Instead, the
compiler forces the programmer to assign values to any local variables
that are used so as to avoid problems associated with mistakenly using
unassigned variables.

```
public class MyApp
{
  int x; // field is assigned default value 0

  int dummy() {
    int x; // local variable must be assigned if used
  }
}
```

Garbage Collector

The Java runtime environment has a garbage collector that periodically
releases the memory used by objects when they're no longer needed.
This frees the programmer from the often tedious and error-prone task
of memory management. An object will be eligible for destruction when
there are no more references to it. This occurs, for example, when the
object goes out of scope. An object can also be explicitly dropped by
setting its references to null.

```java
public class MyApp
{
  public static void main(String[] args)
  {
    MyApp a = new MyApp();

    // Make object available for garbage collection
    a = null;
  }
}
```

CHAPTER 11

Static

The static keyword is used to create fields and methods that can be accessed without having to make an instance of the class. Static (class) members only exist in one copy, which belongs to the class itself, whereas instance (non-static) members are created as new copies for each new object. That means static methods can't use instance members because these methods aren't part of an instance. On the other hand, instance methods can use both static and instance members.

```java
class MyCircle
{
  float r = 10;              // instance field
  static float pi = 3.14F; // static/class field

  // Instance method
  float getArea() { return newArea(r); }

  // Static/class method
  static float newArea(float a) { return pi*a*a; }
}
```

© Mikael Olsson 2022
M. Olsson, *Java 17 Quick Syntax Reference*, https://doi.org/10.1007/978-1-4842-7371-5_11

Accessing Static Members

To access a static member from outside the class, the class name is used followed by the dot operator. This operator is the same as the one used to access instance members, but to reach them, an object reference is required. Trying to access a static member by using an object reference (instead of the class name) will result in a warning since this makes it more difficult to see that a static member is being used.

```java
public static void main(String[] args)
{
  float f = MyCircle.pi;
  MyCircle c = new MyCircle();
  float g = c.r;
}
```

Static Methods

The advantage of static members is that they can be used by other classes without having to create an instance of the class. Fields should therefore be declared static when only a single instance of the variable is needed. Methods should be declared static if they perform a generic function that's independent of any instance variables. A good example of this is the Math class which contains only static methods and fields.

```java
double pi = Math.PI;
```

Math is one of the classes that's included by default in every Java application, because it belongs to the java.lang package, which is always imported. This package contains classes fundamental to the Java language, such as String, Object, and System.

Static Fields

Static fields have the advantage of persisting throughout the life of the application. That means they can be used, for example, to record the number of times a method has been called across all instances of the class. The initial value for a static field will only be set once, sometimes before the class or field is ever used.

```
class MyCircle
{
  static void foo() { count++; }
  static int count = 0;
}
```

Static Initialization Blocks

A *static initialization block* can be used if the initialization of static fields requires more than one line or some other logic. This block, in contrast to the constructor, will only be run once, at the same time as the static fields are initialized.

```
class MyClass
{
  static int[] array = new int[5];

  // Static initialization block
  static
  {
    int i = 0;
    for(int element : array)
      element = i++;
  }
}
```

Instance Initialization Blocks

An *initialization block* provides an alternative method for assigning instance fields. This block is placed on the class level, just like the static initialization block, but without the use of the static keyword. Any code placed between the brackets will be copied to the start of every constructor by the compiler.

```
class MyClass
{
  int[] array = new int[5];

  // Initialization block
  {
    int i = 0;
    for(int element : array) element = i++;
  }
}
```

A class can have multiple instance initialization and static initialization blocks.

CHAPTER 12

Inheritance

Inheritance allows a class to acquire the members of another class. In the following example, Apple inherits from Fruit. This is specified with the extends keyword. Fruit then becomes the superclass of Apple, which in turn becomes a subclass of Fruit. In addition to its own members, Apple gains all accessible members in Fruit, except for any constructors.

```java
// Superclass (parent class)
class Fruit
{
  public String flavor;
}

// Subclass (child class)
class Apple extends Fruit
{
  public String variety;
}
```

A class in Java may only inherit from one superclass, and if no class is specified, it will implicitly inherit from Object. Therefore, Object is the root class of all classes.

```java
// Same as class MyClass {}
class MyClass extends Object {}
```

© Mikael Olsson 2022
M. Olsson, *Java 17 Quick Syntax Reference*, https://doi.org/10.1007/978-1-4842-7371-5_12

Upcasting

Conceptually, a subclass is a specialization of the superclass. This means that Apple is a kind of Fruit, as well as an Object, and can therefore be used anywhere a Fruit or Object is expected. For example, if an instance of Apple is created, it can be *upcast* to Fruit because the subclass contains everything in the superclass.

```
Apple a = new Apple();
Fruit f = a;
```

Through this variable, the Apple is seen as a Fruit, so only the Fruit members can be accessed:

```
f.flavor = "Sweet";
```

Downcasting

When the class is *downcast* back into an Apple, the fields that are specific to Apple will have been preserved. That's because the Fruit only contained the Apple—it didn't convert it to an Apple. The downcast has to be made explicitly using the Java casting format because downcasting an actual Fruit object into an Apple isn't allowed.

```
Apple b = (Apple)f;
```

Instanceof Operator

As a safety precaution, you can make a test during runtime to see whether an object can be cast to a specific class by using the instanceof operator. This operator returns true if the left side object can be cast into the right side type without causing an exception.

```
if (f instanceof Apple)
{
  Apple myApple = (Apple)f;
  // use myApple here
}
```

It is common to use the instanceof operator like this, where the condition check is followed by a type cast. For this reason, a more concise syntax was added where the assigned variable is included in the condition. The scope of the variable is limited to the conditional block only.

```
if (f instanceof Apple myApple)
{
  // use myApple here
}
```

This is part of the *pattern matching* feature of the instanceof operator, which became a preview feature in Java 14 and then a standard feature in Java 16. The operator was extended to take not just a type but to also allow a type to be extracted and tested within a single expression.

```
class Speed
{
  public int velocity = 10;
}

public class MyApp
{
  public static void main(String[] args) {
    Object o = new Speed();
    // ...
    if ( (o instanceof Speed s) && (s.velocity > 5) ) {
      System.out.println("Speed is " + s.velocity);
    }
  }
}
```

Pattern Matching Switch

Java 17 added pattern matching for switch statements and expressions as a preview feature. This extends switch to work with any type pattern, and not just numeric, String, and enum types as was previously the case. When using case labels with patterns, the selection is determined by pattern matching rather than by an equality check. In the following code, the value of the object variable matches the Long pattern, and the code associated with that case will be executed.

```
Object o = 5L; // L suffix means Long type
String myType = switch(o)
{
  case null      -> "null";
  case Integer i -> "integer is " + i;
  case Long l    -> "long is " + l;
  default        -> o.toString();
}
System.out.println(myType) // "long is 5"
```

Restricting Inheritance

A class can be declared as final to prevent any class from inheriting it:

```
// Cannot be inherited
final class Fruit {}
```

A less restrictive method is to use the sealed modifier to only allow inheritance by certain classes. These classes are specified in a comma-separated permits clause placed to the right of any extends clause.

```
// Can be inherited only by Apple or Orange
sealed class Fruit permits Apple, Orange {}
```

Permitted classes that inherit from a sealed class must in turn be declared as non-sealed, sealed, or final. A non-sealed class may be inherited by any class, whereas a final class allows for no more subclasses.

```
// Can be inherited by any class
non-sealed class Lemon extends Fruit{}
```

```
// Can be inherited only by RedDelicious class
sealed class Apple extends Fruit permits RedDelicious{}
```

```
// Cannot be inherited
final class Orange extends Fruit {}
```

Sealed classes were added as a preview feature in Java 15. Both the sealed and final modifiers may also be applied to interfaces and abstract classes.

CHAPTER 13

Overriding

A member in a subclass can redefine a member in its superclass. This is most often done to give instance methods new implementations.

Overriding Methods

In the following example, Rectangle's getArea method is overridden in Triangle by redeclaring it there with the same method signature. The signature includes the name, parameters, and return type of the method. However, the access level may be changed to allow for more access than the method being overridden.

```
class Rectangle
{
  public int w = 10, h = 10;
  public int getArea() { return w * h; }
}

class Triangle extends Rectangle
{
  public int getArea() { return w * h / 2; }
}
```

© Mikael Olsson 2022
M. Olsson, *Java 17 Quick Syntax Reference*, https://doi.org/10.1007/978-1-4842-7371-5_13

Override Annotation

To show that this override was intentional, the @Override annotation
should be placed before the method. This annotation was added in Java 5
to prevent accidental overrides and to improve readability. The compiler
will also give a warning if the annotated method doesn't actually override
anything, which can occur if the signature does not match the method in
the parent class.

```
class Triangle extends Rectangle
{
  @Override
  public int getArea() {
    return w * h / 2;
  }
}
```

Invoking the getArea method from a Triangle instance will call
Triangle's version of the method:

```
Triangle o = new Triangle();
o.getArea(); // (50) calls Triangle's version
```

If Triangle's instance is upcast into Rectangle, then Triangle's
version of the method will still get called because Rectangle's version has
been overridden:

```
Rectangle o = new Triangle();
o.getArea();  // (50) calls Triangle's version
```

Hiding Methods

This is only true for instance methods—not for class (static) methods. If a class method called newArea is added to Rectangle and redefined in Triangle, then Triangle's version of the method will only hide Rectangle's implementation. Because of this, the @Override annotation isn't used.

```
class Rectangle
{
  public int w = 10, h = 10;
  public static int newArea(int a, int b) {
    return a * b;
  }
}

class Triangle extends Rectangle
{
  public static int newArea(int a, int b) {
    return a * b / 2;
  }
}
```

Calling newArea from Triangle's class will, as expected, invoke Triangle's version, but calling the method from Rectangle's class will invoke Rectangle's implementation:

```
Triangle o = new Triangle();
Triangle.newArea(10,10); // (50) calls Triangle's version

Rectangle r = o;
Rectangle.newArea(10,10); // (100) calls Rectangle's version
```

Redefined instance methods will always be overridden in Java, and redefined class methods will always be hidden. There's no way to change this behavior, as can be done in C++ or C#, for example.

Hiding Fields

Fields cannot be overridden in Java, but they can be hidden by declaring a field with the same name as an inherited field. The type of the field and its access level can be different from the inherited field. It is generally not advisable to hide fields, as it makes the code more difficult to read.

```java
class Rectangle
{
  public int w = 10, h = 10;
}

class Triangle extends Rectangle
{
  public int w = 5, h = 5; // hide inherited fields
}

public class MyApp
{
  public static void main(String args[]) {
    Triangle t = new Triangle();
    Rectangle r = t;
    System.out.println(t.w); // "5"
    System.out.println(r.w); // "10"
  }
}
```

Accessing Redefined Members

An overridden method (or hidden instance field) can still be accessed from inside the subclass using the super keyword. This keyword is a reference to the current instance of the superclass.

```
class Triangle extends Rectangle
{
  @Override
  public int getArea() {
    return super.getArea() / 2;
  }
}
```

Calling Parent Constructor

Another place where the super keyword can be used is on the first line of a constructor. There it can perform a method call that invokes the superclass's constructor.

```
public Triangle(int a, int b) { super(a,b); }
```

If the first line of a constructor isn't a call to another constructor, the Java compiler will automatically add a call to the superclass's parameterless constructor. That ensures that all ancestor classes are properly constructed.

```
public Triangle() { super(); }
```

CHAPTER 14

Packages and Import

Packages are used to avoid naming conflicts and to organize code files into different directories. So far in this book, the code file has been located at the root of the project's source directory and has therefore belonged to the so-called *default package*. In Java, the directory a file belongs to, relative to the project's source directory, corresponds to the package name.

To assign a code file to a package—for example, mypackage—it must be moved to a folder by that name, under the project directory. Furthermore, the file must specify which package it belongs to using the package keyword followed by the package name (and path). There may only be one package statement in each source file, and it must be the first line of code, except for any comments. Note that the naming convention for packages is all lowercase.

```
// This file belongs to mypackage
package mypackage;
```

Packages may be any number of directory levels deep, and the levels in the hierarchy are separated by dots. For example, if the mypackage folder containing the code file is placed in a project folder called sub, the package declaration would need to look like this.

```
package sub.mypackage;
```

© Mikael Olsson 2022
M. Olsson, *Java 17 Quick Syntax Reference*, https://doi.org/10.1007/978-1-4842-7371-5_14

Accessing Packages

To illustrate how to access package members, a file named MyClass.java is placed in the sub\mypackage folder under the project's source directory. The file contains a single public class called MyClass.

```
package sub.mypackage;
public class MyClass {}
```

MyClass can be accessed from another source file in one of two ways. The first way is to type the fully qualified name.

```
// Fully qualified class name
sub.mypackage.MyClass m;
```

The second option is to shorten the fully qualified name by including the class with the import keyword. An import statement must be located after the package declaration statement and before all other members in the code file. It has no other purpose than to free the programmer from having to type the fully qualified name.

```
import mypackage.sub.MyClass;
// ...
MyClass m;
```

In addition to importing a specific class, all types (classes or interfaces) inside of a package can be imported by using an asterisk (*). Note that this doesn't import any subpackages.

```
import java.util.*;
```

A third variation of the `import` statement is the static import, which imports all static members of a class. Once the static members are imported, they can be used without having to specify the class name.

```
import static java.lang.Math.*;
// ...
double pi = PI; // Math.PI
```

CHAPTER 15

Modules

A *module* is a reusable group of related packages and resource files together with a module descriptor file. They should be self-sufficient and only expose interfaces to use the module's functionality.

Creating a Module

NetBeans has a special project type for managing multiple modules. To create such a project, go to File ➤ New Project, and from there, select Java Modular Project under the Java with Ant category. Click Next, and give the project the name MyModules, and click Finish to create the project. Go ahead and add a module named "firstmodule" to this project by right-clicking the MyModules item in the Projects window and selecting New ➤ Module.

As can be seen in the Projects window, a module has a special file named module-info.java. This module descriptor file must be located in the root folder of the packages that will be compiled into a module. Inside the file is a module descriptor, which consists of the module keyword followed by the name of the module and a set of curly brackets.

```
module firstmodule {

}
```

© Mikael Olsson 2022
M. Olsson, *Java 17 Quick Syntax Reference*, https://doi.org/10.1007/978-1-4842-7371-5_15

Next, let's create a package with a class to include in this module. Right-click the "firstmodule" item in the Project window, and select New ➤ Java Class. Give it the name util.MyClass to automatically place it in a new Package called util. The package is mandatory since placing files other than the module descriptor in the default package (top-level directory) is not allowed in modules. Type the following code sample into the new source file:

```
// util.MyClass.java
package util;
public class MyClass {
  public static void sayHi() {
    System.out.println("Hello Module");
  }
}
```

Go back to the module descriptor file, and add an export statement for the util package using the exports keyword followed by the fully qualified package name (firstmodule.util). This will make the package visible to any other modules that are using this module. Any other packages, including subpackages, which are not explicitly exported will be inaccessible from outside of the module.

```
module firstmodule {
  exports firstmodule.util; // make package visible
}
```

Using a Module

We will now create a second module to make use of the first module. Add a new module to the project called secondmodule. In its module descriptor file, import firstmodule to make its exported package visible within this new module.

```
module secondmodule {
  requires firstmodule; // import module
}
```

Add a class called app.MyApp to the module, so the class file gets placed in a package called app. Include the following code inside this file which makes use of the util package exposed from the first module:

```
// app.MyApp.java
package app;
public class MyApp {
  public static void main(String[] args) {
    util.MyClass.sayHi(); // "Hello Module"
  }
}
```

This is all the code needed to make the second module use the functionality exposed by the first module. Compile and run the project to have the main method call the function from the imported module, which displays the "Hello Module" text string.

CHAPTER 16

Access Levels

There are four access levels available in Java: public, protected, private, and package-private. Package-private isn't explicitly declared using a keyword. Instead, it's the default access level for every member in Java.

```
public    int myPublic;    // unrestricted access
protected int myProtected;// package or subclass access
          int myPackage;   // package access
private   int myPrivate;  // class access
```

Private Access

All members, regardless of access level, are accessible in the class in which they are declared—the containing class. This is the only place where a private member can be accessed.

```
package mypackage;
public class MyApp
{
  public    int myPublic;
  protected int myProtected;
            int myPackage;
  private   int myPrivate;
```

© Mikael Olsson 2022

M. Olsson, *Java 17 Quick Syntax Reference*, https://doi.org/10.1007/978-1-4842-7371-5_16

```
  void test()
  {
    myPublic   = 0; // allowed
    myProtected = 0; // allowed
    myPackage   = 0; // allowed
    myPrivate   = 0; // allowed
  }
}
```

Package-Private Access

Package-private members can be accessed anywhere within the containing package, but not from another package:

```
package mypackage;
public class MyClass
{
  void test(MyApp m)
  {
    m.myPublic   = 0; // allowed
    m.myProtected = 0; // allowed
    m.myPackage   = 0; // allowed
    m.myPrivate   = 0; // inaccessible
  }
}
```

Protected Access

Protected members are accessible within subclasses and within the
containing package. In the following code, the protected member can be
accessed because MyChild it is a subclass of MyApp which defines that
member:

```
package newpackage;
import mypackage.MyApp;

public class MyChild extends MyApp
{
  void test()
  {
    myPublic    = 0; // allowed
    myProtected = 0; // allowed (in subclass)
    myPackage   = 0; // inaccessible
    myPrivate   = 0; // inaccessible
  }
}
```

Note that in addition to subclasses, protected members are also
accessible anywhere within the containing package. This behavior is
different from other languages, such as C++ and C#, where protected
members are only accessible from subclasses and the containing class.

```
package mypackage;
public class MyTest
{
  void test(MyApp m)
  {
    m.myPublic    = 0; // allowed
    m.myProtected = 0; // allowed (same package)
```

81

```
    m.myPackage   = 0; // inaccessible
    m.myPrivate   = 0; // inaccessible
  }
}
```

Public Access

The public modifier gives unrestricted access from anywhere the member can be referenced:

```
package newpackage;
import mypackage.MyApp;

public class MyClass
{
  void test(MyApp m)
  {
    m.myPublic    = 0; // allowed
    m.myProtected = 0; // inaccessible
    m.myPackage   = 0; // inaccessible
    m.myPrivate   = 0; // inaccessible
  }
}
```

Top-Level Access

Members declared directly in the package—top-level members—may only choose between package-private and public access. For instance, a top-level class without an access modifier will default to package-private. Such a class will only be accessible within the containing package. In contrast, a top-level class explicitly declared as public can be reached from other packages as well.

```
// Accessible only from containing package
class PackagePrivateClass {}

// Accessible from any package
public class PublicClass {}
```

Nested Class Access

Java allows classes to be defined within other classes, and these are called *nested classes*. Such a class can have any one of the four access levels. If a nested class is made inaccessible, it can't be instantiated or inherited.

```
public class MyClass
{
  // Only accessible within MyClass
  private class PrivateNestedClass {}
}
```

Keep in mind that nested members can be restricted by both their own access level and that of the containing class. For instance, a public nested class inside of a package-private class won't be accessible from other packages.

```
class MyClass
{
  // Only accessible within containing package
  public class PrivateNestedClass {}
}
```

Access-Level Guideline

As a guideline, when choosing an access level, it's generally best to use the most restrictive level possible. That's because the more places a member can be accessed, the more places it can be accessed incorrectly, which makes the code harder to debug. Using restrictive access levels also makes it easier to modify the class without breaking the code for any other developers using that class.

CHAPTER 17

Constants

A variable in Java can be made into a constant by adding the final keyword before the data type. This modifier means that the variable can't be reassigned once it's been set, and any attempts to do so will result in a compile-time error.

Local Constants

A local variable can instead be declared as a constant by applying the final keyword. Such a constant must always be initialized at the same time as it's declared. The Java naming convention for constants is to use all uppercase letters and to separate words with underscores.

```
final double PI = 3.14;
```

Constant Fields

Class and instance variables can be declared as final, as seen in the following example:

```
class MyClass
{
  final double E = 2.72;
  static final double C = 3e8;
  final static double D = 1.23; // alternative order
}
```

© Mikael Olsson 2022
M. Olsson, *Java 17 Quick Syntax Reference*, https://doi.org/10.1007/978-1-4842-7371-5_17

In contrast to local constants, *constant* fields don't have to be assigned at declaration. A constant instance field can optionally be assigned in a constructor or an instance initialization block, whereas a constant static field may be assigned by using a static initialization block. These alternative assignments can be useful if the constant's value needs to be calculated and doesn't fit on a single code line.

```
class MyClass
{
  final double E;
  final double PI;
  static final double C;

  public MyClass() { E = 2.72; }
  { PI = 3.14; }
  static { C = 3e8; }
}
```

Constant Method Parameters

Another place where the final modifier may be applied is to method parameters to make them unchangeable. Doing so provides a signal to other developers that the method won't modify the argument passed to it.

```
void f(final String A) {}
```

Compile-Time and Runtime Constants

Like most other languages, Java has both compile-time and runtime constants. However, only class constants can be compile-time constants in Java and only if their value is known at compilation. All other uses of final will create runtime constants. With compile-time constants, the compiler will replace the constant name everywhere in the code with its value. These are therefore faster than runtime constants, which aren't set until the program is run. Runtime constants, though, can be assigned dynamic values that can be different from one program run to the next.

```java
class MyClass
{
  // Compile-time constant (static and known at compile-time)
  final static double C = 3e8;

  // Run-time constant (not static)
  final double E = 2.72;

  // Run-time constant (not known at compile-time)
  final static int RND = (new
  java.util.Random()).nextInt();
}
```

Constant Guideline

In general, it's a good idea to always declare variables as final, and constant fields as static final, if they don't need to be reassigned. That ensures that the fields and variables won't be changed anywhere in the program by mistake, which in turn helps prevent bugs.

CHAPTER 18

Interface

The interface type is used to specify methods that classes using the interface must implement. These methods are created with the interface keyword followed by a name and a code block. Their naming convention is the same as for classes, with the first letter of each word capitalized.

```
interface MyInterface {}
```

When an interface isn't nested inside another type, its access level can be either package-private or public, just like any other top-level member.

Interface Members

The code block for an interface can, first of all, contain signatures for instance methods. These methods don't have any implementations. Instead, their bodies are replaced by semicolons. Interface members have public access by default, so this modifier can be left out.

```
interface MyInterface {
  int myMethod(); // method signature
}
```

© Mikael Olsson 2022
M. Olsson, *Java 17 Quick Syntax Reference*, https://doi.org/10.1007/978-1-4842-7371-5_18

The second member that an interface can contain is constants. Any field created in an interface will be implicitly declared as static final, so these modifiers can also be left out.

```
interface MyInterface {
  int c = 10; // constant
}
```

In addition to method signatures and constants, an interface can also contain nested containing types, such as classes or other interfaces:

```
interface MyInterface
{
  // Types
  class Class {}
  interface Interface {}
  enum Enum {}
}
```

Interface Example

The following example shows an interface called Comparable, which has a single method named compare:

```
interface Comparable
{
  int compare(Object o);
}
```

The following class implements this interface using the `implements` keyword after the class name. By convention, the implements clause is placed after the `extends` clause if the class has one. Note that although a class can only inherit from one superclass, it may implement any number of interfaces by specifying them in a comma-separated list.

```
class Circle implements Comparable
{
  public int r;
  // ...
}
```

Because `Circle` implements `Comparable`, it must define the `compare` method. For this class, the method will return the difference between the circle radiuses. The implemented method must be public and must have the same signature as the method defined in the interface.

```
class Circle implements Comparable
{
  public int r;

  @Override
  public int compare(Object o) {
    return r - ( (Circle)o ).r;
  }
}
```

Functionality Interface

`Comparable` demonstrates the first use of interfaces, which is to define a specific functionality that classes can share. It makes it possible to use the interface members without having to know the actual type of a class, a concept called polymorphism. To illustrate, the next example shows a simple method that takes two `Comparable` objects and returns the largest one. This method will work for any class that implements the `Comparable` interface because the method only uses the functionality exposed through that interface.

```
public static Object largest(Comparable a, Comparable b)
{
  return (a.compare(b) > 0) ? a : b;
}
```

Class Interface

A second way to use an interface is to provide an actual interface for a class, through which the class can be used. The following example defines an interface for `MyClass` called `MyInterface`. This interface only includes the functionality that programmers using `MyClass` may need.

```
interface MyInterface
{
  void exposed();
}

class MyClass implements MyInterface
{
  @Override
  public void exposed() {}
  public void hidden() {}
}
```

The interface type is then used to hold the implementing class, so the class is only seen through this interface:

```
public static void main(String[] args)
{
  MyInterface i = new MyClass();
}
```

This abstraction provides two benefits. First, it makes it easier for other programmers to use the class because they now only have access to the methods that are relevant. Second, it makes the class more flexible because its implementation can change, without being noticeable by other programmers using the class, as long as the interface is followed.

Interface Classes

As mentioned, an interface can contain nested types, such as classes. In contrast to methods, these types are implemented inside the interface. This can, for example, be used to provide a class that contains static methods useful for implementing classes. These nested types are only visible to classes implementing the interface and not to objects of those classes.

```
interface MyInterface
{
  class HelperClass {
    public static void helperMethod() {}
  }
}
```

Default Interface Methods

Java 8 added the ability to define default methods in interfaces. Such a method is specified using the default keyword and can then include an implementation inside the interface.

```
interface MyInterface
{
  default void defaultMethod() {
    System.out.println("default");
  }
}
```

   A default method will be used unless it's overridden by an implementing class. This provides a backward-compatible way to add new methods to an interface without breaking existing classes that use the interface.

```
public class MyApp implements MyInterface
{
  public static void main(String[] args) {
    MyInterface i = new MyApp();
    i.defaultMethod(); // "default"
  }
}
```

Static Interface Methods

Another feature introduced in Java 8 was static interface methods. Similar to static class methods, these methods belong to the interface and can only be called from an interface context.

```java
interface MyInterface
{
  public static void staticMethod() {
    System.out.println("static");
  }
}

class MyApp
{
  public static void main(String[] args) {
    MyInterface.staticMethod(); // "static"
  }
}
```

As of Java 9, static interface methods can have private access. This enables lengthy default interface methods to be split across private static interface methods, which allows for less code duplication.

```java
interface MyInterface
{
  private static String getString() {
    return "string";
  }

  default void printString() {
    System.out.println(getString());
  }
}
```

CHAPTER 19

Abstract

An *abstract* class provides a partial implementation that other classes can build upon. When a class is declared abstract, it means it can contain incomplete methods that must be implemented in subclasses, in addition to normal class members. These methods are left unimplemented and only specify their signatures, while their bodies are replaced by semicolons.

```java
abstract class Shape
{
  public int x = 100, y = 100;
  public abstract int getArea();
}
```

Abstract Class Example

If a class called Rectangle inherits from the abstract class Shape, Rectangle is then forced to override the abstract getArea method. The only exception is if Rectangle is also declared abstract, in which case it doesn't have to implement any abstract methods.

```java
class Rectangle extends Shape
{
  @Override public int getArea() {
    return x * y;
  }
}
```

An abstract class can't be instantiated, but it can be used to hold instances of its subclasses:

```
public class MyApp
{
  public static void main(String[] args) {
    Shape s = new Rectangle();
  }
}
```

Even though an abstract class can't be instantiated, it may have constructors, which can be called from the subclass's constructors using the super keyword:

```
abstract class Shape
{
  public int x = 100, y = 100;
  public Shape(int a, int b) {
    x = a;
    y = b;
  }
}

class Rectangle extends Shape
{
  public Rectangle(int a, int b) {
    super(a,b);
  }
}
```

```
public class MyApp
{
  public static void main(String[] args) {
    Rectangle s = new Rectangle(5, 10);
  }
}
```

Abstract Classes and Interfaces

Abstract classes are similar to interfaces in many ways. They can both define method signatures that subclasses must implement, and neither one of them can be instantiated. One key difference is that an abstract class can contain any abstract or non-abstract member, whereas an interface is limited to abstract members, nested types, and static constants, as well as static methods, default methods, and private methods. Another difference is that a class can implement any number of interfaces but only inherit from one class, abstract or not.

An interface is either used to define a specific functionality that a class can have or to provide an interface for other developers using a class. In contrast, an abstract class is used to provide a partial class implementation, leaving it up to subclasses to complete it. This is useful when subclasses have some functionality in common but also have some functionality that must be implemented differently for each subclass.

CHAPTER 20

Enum

An *enumeration*, or *enum*, is a type that consists of a fixed list of named constants. To create one, the enum keyword is used followed by a name and a code block containing a comma-separated list of constant elements. The access level for an enum is the same as for a class. Package-private by default, but it can also be set to public if it's declared in a file of the same name. As with classes, an enum can also be contained within a class, where it can then be set to any access level.

```java
enum Speed
{
  STOP, SLOW, NORMAL, FAST
}
```

An object of the enum type just shown can hold any one of the four defined constants. The enum constants are accessed as if they were static fields of a class.

```java
Speed s = Speed.SLOW;
```

The switch statement provides a good example of when an enumeration can be useful. Compared to using ordinary constants, an enum has the advantage of allowing the programmer to clearly specify

© Mikael Olsson 2022
M. Olsson, *Java 17 Quick Syntax Reference*, https://doi.org/10.1007/978-1-4842-7371-5_20

what constant values are allowed. This provides compile-time type safety. Note that when using an enum in a `switch` statement, the case labels aren't qualified with the name of the enum.

```
public class MyApp
{
  public static void main(String args[]) {
    Speed s = Speed.NORMAL;
    // ...
    switch(s) {
      case STOP: break;
      case SLOW: break;
      case NORMAL: break;
      case FAST: break;
    }
  }
}
```

Enum Class

In Java, the enum type is more powerful than its counterparts in other languages, such as C++ or C#. Essentially a special kind of class, it can include anything a class can include. To add a class member, the list of constants must be terminated with a semicolon, and the member must be declared after the constants. In the following example, an integer is added to the enum, which will hold the actual speed that the elements represent.

```
enum Speed
{
  STOP, SLOW, NORMAL, FAST;
  public int velocity;
  // ...
}
```

To set this field, a constructor needs to be added as well. A constructor in an enum is always private and isn't called in the same way as for a regular class. Instead, the parameters to the constructor are given after the constant elements, as seen in the next example. If a Speed enum object is assigned the constant SLOW, then the argument 5 will be passed to the constructor for that enum instance.

```
enum Speed
{
  STOP(0), SLOW(5), NORMAL(10), FAST(20);
  public int velocity;
  private Speed(int s) { velocity = s; }
}

public class MyApp
{
  public static void main(String args[]) {
    Speed s = Speed.SLOW;
    System.out.println(s.velocity); // "5"
  }
}
```

Another difference that enum types have when compared to regular classes is that they implicitly extend from the java.lang.Enum class. In addition to the members inherited from this class, the compiler will also automatically add two static methods to the enumeration, namely, *values* and *valueof*. The values method returns an array of the constant elements declared in the enum, and valueof returns the enum constant of the specified enum name.

```
Speed[] a = Speed.values();
String s = a[0].toString(); // "STOP"
Speed b = Speed.valueOf(s); // Speed.STOP
```

CHAPTER 21

Exception Handling

Exception handling allows programmers to deal with unexpected situations that may occur in their programs. For example, the FileReader class in the java.io package is used to open a file. Creating an instance of this class will cause the IDE to give a reminder that the class's constructor may throw a FileNotFoundException. Attempting to run the program will also cause the compiler to point this out.

```java
import java.io.*;
public class MyClass
{
  public static void main(String[] args)
  {
    // Compile-time error
    FileReader file = new FileReader("missing.txt");
  }
}
```

Try-Catch

To handle this compile-time error, the exception must be caught by using a try-catch statement. This statement consists of a try block containing the code that may cause the exceptions and one or more catch clauses. If the try block executes successfully, the program will continue running after the try-catch statement, but if an exception occurs, execution will then be passed to the first catch block able to handle that exception type.

```
try {
    FileReader file = new FileReader("missing.txt");
}
catch(FileNotFoundException e) {}
```

Catch Block

In the preceding example, the catch block is only set to handle the FileNotFoundException. If the code in the try block could throw more kinds of exceptions, and all of them should be handled in the same way, a more general exception can be caught instead, such as the Exception class itself from which all exceptions derive. This catch clause would then be able to handle all the exceptions that inherit from this class, including the FileNotFoundException. Bear in mind that a more general exception needs to be caught after a more specific exception. The catch clause must always define an exception object. This object can be used to obtain more information about the exception, such as a description of the exception using the getMessage method.

```
catch(FileNotFoundException e) {
    System.out.print(e.getMessage());
}
catch(Exception e) {
    System.out.print(e.getMessage());
}
```

As of Java 7, multiple exceptions of different types can be caught using a single catch block. This helps avoid code duplication, without having to catch an overly general exception type, in cases when multiple exceptions are to be handled in the same way. Each exception is separated with a vertical bar (|) in the catch clause.

```
catch(IOException | SQLException e) {
  // Handle exception
}
```

Finally Block

As the last clause in a try-catch statement, a finally block can be added. This block is used to clean up resources allocated in the try block and will always execute whether or not there's an exception. In this example, the file opened in the try block should be closed, but only if it was successfully opened. To be able to access the FileReader object from the finally clause, it must be declared outside of the try block. Additionally, because the close method can also throw an exception, the method needs to be surrounded with another try-catch block. Keep in mind that if you forget to close a resource object, Java's garbage collector will eventually close the resource for you, but closing it yourself is good programming practice.

```
FileReader file = null;
try {
  file = new FileReader("missing.txt");
}
catch(FileNotFoundException e) {
  System.out.print(e.getMessage());
}
```

```
finally {
  if (file != null) {
    try { file.close(); }
    catch(IOException e) {}
  }
}
```

Java 7 added the try-with-resources feature. This feature allows resource objects to be automatically closed by defining the resource object in parentheses after the `try` keyword. For this to work, the resource must implement the `java.lang.AutoClosable` interface. This interface consists of only the `close` method, which is called automatically in an implicit `finally` statement. The preceding example can therefore be simplified as follows:

```
try(FileReader file = new FileReader("missing.txt")) {
  // Read file
}
catch(FileNotFoundException e) {
  // Handle exception
}
```

More than one resource object can be included for automatic closing, separated with a semicolon. To improve readability, Java 9 made it possible for objects declared outside of the parentheses to be referenced for the try-with-resources statement, provided these resources are final or effectively final.

```
// Final resource
final FileReader file1 = new FileReader("file1.txt");

// Effectively final resource (never changed)
FileReader file2 = new FileReader("file2.txt");

try(file1; file2) {
  // Read files
}
```

```
catch(FileNotFoundException e) {
  // Handle exception
}
```

Throwing Exceptions

When a situation occurs that a method can't recover from, it can generate its own exception to signal to the caller that the method has failed. It does that using the throw keyword followed by a new instance of a Throwable type.

```
static void makeException()
{
  throw new Throwable("My Throwable");
}
```

Checked and Unchecked Exceptions

Exceptions in Java are grouped into two categories—checked and unchecked—depending on whether or not they need to be specified. A method that throws a checked exception—for example, IOException—will not compile unless it's specified using a throws clause after the method's parameter list and the calling method catches the exception. Unchecked exceptions, on the other hand, such as the ArithmeticException, do not have to be caught or specified. Note that to specify multiple exceptions, the exception types are separated by a comma.

```
static void MakeException()
throws IOException, FileNotFoundException
{
  // ...
```

```
throw new IOException("My IO exception");
// ...
throw new FileNotFoundException("File missing");
}
```

Exception Hierarchy

Exceptions, like most everything else in Java, are classes that exist in a hierarchy. At the root of this hierarchy (below `Object`) is the `Throwable` class, and all descendants of this class can be both thrown and caught. Inheriting from `Throwable` are the `Error` and `Exception` classes. Classes descending from `Error` are used to indicate non-recoverable exceptions, such as the `OutOfMemoryError`. These are unchecked because once they've occurred, it's unlikely that the programmer can do anything about them even if they're caught.

Descending from `Exception` are the `RuntimeExceptions`, which are also unchecked. These are exceptions that can occur in almost any code, and it would therefore be cumbersome to catch and specify them. For example, a division by zero will throw an `ArithmeticException`, but surrounding every division operation with a `try-catch` would be bothersome. There's also some overhead associated with checking for exceptions, and the cost of checking for these exceptions typically outweighs the benefit of catching them. The other `Exception` descendants, those that don't inherit from `RuntimeExceptions`, are all checked. These are exceptions that can be recovered from and that must be both caught and specified.

CHAPTER 22

Boxing and Unboxing

Placing a primitive variable in an object is known as *boxing*. Boxing allows the primitive to be used where objects are required. For this purpose, Java provides wrapper classes to implement boxing for each primitive type—namely, Byte, Short, Integer, Long, Float, Double, Character, and Boolean. An Integer object, for example, can hold a variable of the type int.

```
int iPrimitive = 5;
Integer iWrapper = new Integer(iPrimitive); // boxing
```

The opposite of boxing is, naturally, *unboxing*, which converts the object type back into its primitive type.

```
iPrimitive = iWrapper.intValue(); // unboxing
```

The wrapper classes belong to the java.lang package, which is always imported. When using wrapper objects, keep in mind that the equal to operator (==) checks whether both references refer to the same object, whereas the equals method is used to compare the values that the objects represent.

```
Integer x = new Integer(1000);
Integer y = new Integer(1000);
boolean b = (x == y);      // false
        b = x.equals(y); // true
```

© Mikael Olsson 2022
M. Olsson, *Java 17 Quick Syntax Reference*, https://doi.org/10.1007/978-1-4842-7371-5_22

Autoboxing and Autounboxing

Java 5 introduced *autoboxing* and *autounboxing*. These features allow for automatic conversion between primitives and their wrapper objects.

```
Integer iWrapper = iPrimitive; // autoboxing
iPrimitive = iWrapper;         // autounboxing
```

Note that this is only syntactic sugar designed to make the code easier to read. The compiler will add the necessary code to box and unbox the primitives for you, using the valueOf and intValue methods.

```
Integer iWrapper = Integer.valueOf(iPrimitive);
iPrimitive = iWrapper.intValue()
```

Primitive and Wrapper Guideline

Primitive types should be used when there's no need for objects. That's because primitives are generally faster and more memory efficient than objects. Conversely, wrappers are useful when numerical values are needed but objects are required. For example, to store numerical values in a collection class, such as ArrayList<>, the wrapper classes are needed.

```
import java.util.ArrayList;
// ...
java.util.ArrayList<Integer> a = new java.util.ArrayList<>();
a.add(10); // autoboxing
int i = a.get(0); // autounboxing
```

Bear in mind that conversions between primitives and wrapper objects should be kept low if speed is important. There's an inherit performance penalty associated with any boxing and unboxing operation.

CHAPTER 23

Generics

Generics refers to the use of type parameters, which provide a way to define methods, classes, and interfaces that can operate with different data types. The benefits of generics are that they provide compile-time type safety and they eliminate the need for most type conversions.

Generic Classes

Generic classes allow class members to use type parameters. Such a class is defined by adding a type parameter section after the class name, which contains a type parameter enclosed between angle brackets. The naming convention for type parameters is that they should consist of a single uppercase letter. Typically, the letter T for *type* is used. The following example defines a generic container class that can hold a single element of the generic type:

```
// Generic container class
class MyBox<T> { public T box; }
```

When an object of this generic class is instantiated, the type parameter must be replaced with an actual data type, such as Integer:

```
MyBox<Integer> iBox = new MyBox<Integer>();
```

© Mikael Olsson 2022
M. Olsson, *Java 17 Quick Syntax Reference*, https://doi.org/10.1007/978-1-4842-7371-5_23

Alternatively, as of Java 7, a generic class can be instantiated with an empty set of type parameters. This type of instantiation is possible as long as the compiler can infer (determine) the type parameters from the context.

```
MyBox<Integer> iBox = new MyBox<>();
```

When an instance of MyBox is created, each type parameter in the class definition is replaced with the passed-in type argument. The object therefore behaves as a regular object, with a single field of the Integer type.

```
iBox.box = 5;
Integer i = iBox.box;
```

Notice that no casting is required when the stored value is set or retrieved from the box field. Furthermore, if the generic field is mistakenly assigned to or set to an incompatible type, the compiler will point that out.

```
iBox.box = "Hello World"; // compile-time error
String s = iBox.box;      // compile-time error
```

Generic Methods

A method can be made generic by declaring it with a type parameter section before the method's return type. The type parameter can be used like any other type inside of the method. You can also use it for the method's return type, in the throws clause and for its parameter types. The next example shows a generic class method that accepts a generic array parameter, the content of which is printed out.

```
class MyClass
{
  public static <T> void printArray(T[] array)
```

```
  {
    for (T element : array)
      System.out.println(element);
  }
}
```

The preceding shown class isn't generic. Methods can be declared as generic, independently of whether or not the enclosing class or interface is generic. The same is true for constructors, as seen in the following example:

```
public class MyApp
{
  private String s;

  public <T> MyApp(T t) {
    s = t.toString(); // convert to string
  }

  public static void main(String[] args) {
    MyApp o = new MyApp(10);
    System.out.println(o.s); // "10"
  }
}
```

Calling Generic Methods

A generic method is typically invoked just as a regular (non-generic) method, without specifying the type argument:

```
Integer[] iArray = { 1, 2, 3 };
MyClass.printArray(iArray);
```

In most cases, the Java compiler can infer the type argument of a generic method call, so it doesn't have to be included. But if that's not the case, then the type argument will need to be explicitly specified before the method name:

```
MyClass.<Integer>printArray(iArray);
```

Generic Interfaces

Interfaces that are declared with type parameters become generic interfaces. Generic interfaces have the same two purposes as regular interfaces: they're either created to expose members of a class that will be used by other classes or to force a class to implement a specific functionality. When a generic interface is implemented, the type argument must be specified. The generic interface can be implemented by both generic and non-generic classes:

```
// Generic functionality interface
interface IGenericCollection<T>
{
  void store(T t);
}

// Non-generic class implementing generic interface
class Box implements IGenericCollection<Integer>
{
  private Integer myBox;
  public void store(Integer i) { myBox = i; }
}
```

```
// Generic class implementing generic interface
class GenericBox<T> implements IGenericCollection<T>
{
  private T myBox;
  public void store(T t) { myBox = t; }
}
```

Generic Type Parameters

The passed-in type argument for a generic can either be a class type, interface type, or another generic type parameter, but it can't be a primitive type. Generics can have more than one type parameter defined, by adding more of them between the angle brackets in a comma-separated list. Bear in mind that each parameter within the brackets must be unique.

```
class MyClass<T, U> {}
```

If a generic has multiple type parameters defined, the same number of type arguments need to be specified when the generic is used.

```
MyClass<Integer, Float> m = new MyClass<>();
```

Generic Variable Usages

Generics are only a compile-time construct in Java. After the compiler has checked that the types used with generic variables are correct, it will then erase all type parameter and argument information from the generic code and insert the appropriate casts instead. That means generics don't provide any performance benefits over non-generic code, because of removed runtime casts, as they do in, for example, C#. It also means generic types can't be used for anything that requires runtime information—such as creating new instances of generic types or using the `instanceof` operator with type parameters. Operations that are allowed include declaring variables of the generic type, assigning null to generic variables, and calling `Object` methods.

```
class MyClass<T>
{
  public void myMethod(Object o)
  {
    T t1;                                 // allowed
    t1 = null;                            // allowed
    System.out.print(t1.toString());      // allowed
    if (o instanceof T) {}                // invalid
    T t2 = new T();                       // invalid
  }
}
```

The process of removing type information from generic code is known as *type erasure*. For example, `MyBox<Integer>` would be reduced to `MyBox`, which is called the *raw type*. This step is performed in order to maintain backward compatibility with code written before generics became part of the language in Java 5.

Bounded Type Parameters

It's possible to apply compile-time enforced restrictions on the kinds of type parameters that a generic may be used with. These restrictions, called *bounds*, are specified within the type parameter section using the `extends` keyword. Type parameters can be bounded by either superclass or interface. For example, the following class B may only be instantiated with a type argument that's either of the type A or has that class as a superclass.

```
// T must be or inherit from A
class B<T extends A> {}
class A {}
```

The next example specifies an interface as the bound. This will restrict the type parameter to only those types that implement the specified interface or are of the interface type itself.

```
// T must be or implement interface I
class C<T extends I> {}
interface I {}
```

Multiple bounds can be applied to a type parameter by specifying them in a list separated by ampersands:

```
class D<T extends A & I> {}
```

The ampersand acts as the separator instead of a comma because comma is already used for separating type parameters:

```
class E<T extends A & I, U extends A & I> {}
```

Aside from restricting the use of a generic to only certain parameter types, another reason for applying bounds is to increase the number of permitted method calls supported by the bounded type. An unbounded type may only call the Object methods. However, by applying a superclass or interface bound, the accessible members of that type will also become available.

```
class Fruit
{
  public String name;
}

class FruitBox<T extends Fruit>
{
  private T box;
  public void FruitBox(T t) { box = t; }
  public String getFruitName()
```

```
    {
        // Use of Fruit member allowed since T extends Fruit
        return box.name;
    }
}
```

Generics and Object

Before generics were introduced in Java 5, the Object type was used to create container classes that could store any type of objects. As generics were made available, this use of the Object type as a universal container should be avoided. That's because the compiler helps ensure that generics are type safe at compile time, which can't be done when using the Object type.

The collection classes in the Java library, among them ArrayList, have all been replaced with generic versions. Even so, any generic class can still be used as if it weren't generic, simply by leaving out the type argument section. The default Object type will then be used as the type argument. That's why the non-generic version of ArrayList is still allowed. Consider the following use of a non-generic ArrayList:

```
import java.util.ArrayList;
// ...
// Object ArrayList
ArrayList a = new ArrayList();
a.add("Hello World");
// ...
Integer b = (Integer)a.get(0); // run-time error
```

This String-to-Integer conversion will fail at runtime by throwing a ClassCastException. Had a generic ArrayList been used instead, the mistaken conversion would have been detected upon compilation, or immediately in an IDE such as NetBeans. This compile-time debugging feature is a major advantage with using generics over other coding approaches.

```
import java.util.ArrayList;
// ...
// Generic ArrayList (recommended)
ArrayList<String> a = new ArrayList<>();
a.add("Hello World");
// ...
Integer b = (Integer)a.get(0); // compile-time error
```

With the generic alternative, only the specified type argument will be allowed into the ArrayList collection. Additionally, values obtained from the collection don't have to be cast to the correct type because the compiler takes care of that.

CHAPTER 24

Lambda Expressions

Java 8 introduced the *lambda expression*, which provides a concise way to represent a method using an expression. A lambda expression consists of three parts: an argument list, the arrow operator (->), and a body. The following lambda takes two integer arguments and returns their sum.

```
(int x, int y) -> { return x + y; };
```

The parameter types generally don't need to be specified because the compiler can determine these types automatically. This type inference also applies to the return type. If the body contains only a single statement, you can leave out the curly brackets, and the result of the statement will then be returned.

```
(x, y) -> x + y;
```

Lambda Objects

A lambda expression is a representation of a *functional interface*, which is an interface defining a single abstract method. It can therefore be bound to an object of such an interface provided that its functional method has a matching signature.

```
interface Summable
{
  public int combine(int a, int b);
}
```

© Mikael Olsson 2022
M. Olsson, *Java 17 Quick Syntax Reference*, https://doi.org/10.1007/978-1-4842-7371-5_24

```java
public class MyApp
{
  public static void main(String[] args) {
    Summable s = (x, y) -> x + y;
    s.combine(2, 3); // 5
}
```

Common functional interfaces are defined in the java.util.function package added in Java 8. In this example, the BinaryOperator<T> interface can be used. It represents a method that takes two arguments and returns a result of the same type as the arguments. Its functional method is named apply.

```java
import java.util.function.*;
public class MyApp
{
  public static void main(String[] args) {
    BinaryOperator<Integer> adder = (x, y) -> x + y;
    adder.apply(2, 3); // 5
  }
}
```

When working on a single operand and returning a value of the same type, you can use the UnaryOperator functional interface. Note that the parentheses surrounding the parameters can be left out when there's only one parameter.

```java
UnaryOperator<Integer> doubler = x -> x*2;
doubler.apply(2); // 4
```

Lambda Parameters

Unlike methods, lambda expressions don't belong to any class. They're objects in and of themselves as they're instances of functional interfaces. A benefit of this is that they provide a convenient way to pass functionality as an argument to another method. In the following example, the Runnable interface is used, which has a functional method that takes no parameters and returns no value. This interface belongs to java.lang, and its abstract method is named run.

```
public class MyApp
{
  static void starter(Runnable s) { s.run(); }

  public static void main(String[] args) {
    Runnable r = () -> System.out.println("Hello");
    starter(r); // "Hello"
  }
}
```

You can also achieve this functionality by defining an anonymous (unnamed) inner class, but this approach is considerably more verbose than the lambda expression.

```
Runnable r = new Runnable() {
  @Override public void run() {
    System.out.println("Hello");
  }
};
starter(r); // "Hello"
```

A lambda expression can capture variables from its context, provided that the referenced variable is final or effectively final (only assigned once). In this next example, the Consumer functional interface is used, which represents a function that accepts one parameter and returns no value.

```
import java.util.function.*;
public class MyApp
{
  final static String GREETING = "Hi ";

  public static void main(String[] args) {
    Consumer<String> c = (s) ->
      System.out.println(GREETING + s);
    c.accept("John"); // "Hi John"
  }
}
```

Behind the scenes, the compiler will instantiate an anonymous class containing a single method to represent a lambda expression. That enables lambdas to be fully backward compatible with earlier versions of the Java runtime environment.

Index

Symbols

dot operator (.), 3
Concatenation operator (+), 21
Increment (++) and decrement
(−−) operators, 16
Assignment operator (=), 10

A

Abstract class
definition, 97
example, 97, 98
interfaces, 99
Access levels
definition, 79
guideline, 84
nested class, 83
package-private, 80
private, 79
protected members, 81
public modifiers, 82
top-level access, 83
app.MyApp, 77
Array
allocation, 27
ArrayList class, 29
assignment, 28

declaration, 27
definition, 27
multidimensional, 28
Autoboxing and autounboxing, 112

B

Bitwise operators, 18
Boxing, 111
break keyword, 33, 39

C

Class
accessing object members, 48
constructor, 49
constructor chaining, 51
constructor overloading, 50, 51
default constructor, 52
default values, 53
definition, 47
garbage collector, 53
invalid field values, 51
null, 52
object creation, 47, 48
Compile/run
comments, 6, 7
console window, 5, 6

© Mikael Olsson 2022
M. Olsson, *Java 17 Quick Syntax Reference*, https://doi.org/10.1007/978-1-4842-7371-5

Printed in the United States
by Baker & Taylor Publisher Services